Moscow Story

My story of the 1980 Moscow Olympic Boycott

By

Brian Newth

WPRR Publishing

Acknowledgements:

1980 Olympic Opening march and 1980 NZ Team photos from Roberts Photography

Photos of the author running and riding we clippings taken from Wellington Newspapers 1978/79

ISBN: 978-0-473-40283-9

Contents

Editor's note

My introduction as a child to the spectacle of sport was through the Olympic Games. My earliest memories are of the Munich Games in 1972 when I was only four years old, partly engrained because of the tragedy that occurred there but also because my family had visited the Olympic complex when we were touring Europe, only weeks before the games commenced.

But it was 1976 Montreal Games, the first to be broadcast live on NZ television via satellite, that really fired my imagination. For two weeks, our school classroom hummed with excitement as we collectively shared the joy of Nadia Comaneci's legendary 'perfect 10', the NZ hockey team's victory over Australia and John Walker's extraordinary gold medal winning performance in the 1500m.

Four years later I was looking forward to experiencing that buzz again, only to discover that nearly half the world's nations wouldn't be attending, there would be no TV coverage, and news about the event would be restricted to short articles in the daily newspapers. It was so disappointing.

Twenty-one years later I met Brian when I joined the Wellington Pistol Club. Encouraged by his optimism and coaching ability, he was my 'go-to guy' for advice in my new sport which I had discovered with a relish. I recall hearing how he had attended the 1980 Olympics and the penny began to drop… oh… that Olympics.

Brian's story is extraordinary and to have been involved in helping him tell it has been an honour. It's an account of a man who stood up and fought for what he knew to be right; it's an example to us all.

Gábor Tóth

Introduction

I've waited 37 years to tell this story.

In 1980 one of the greatest disgraces ever to have occurred in New Zealand sport took place; the near-complete boycott of the Moscow Olympic Games. All but two of the smallest sports agreed to the boycott despite all of the country's Olympic affiliated organisations having agreed to abide by the Olympic Charter, rule 24c of which stated;

"National Olympic committees must be autonomous and must resist all pressures of any kind whatsoever, whether of a political, religious or economic nature".

Only four competitors and four officials out of the original team of one hundred and twenty refused to be intimidated and bullied into joining the boycott.

I was one of them.

It's history now but I believe history should be about the truth. Everything in this story happened though some people may find this difficult to accept. Prior to my experiences around the 1980 Olympic Games, I believed in the myth that New Zealand was a land of rugged individuals ready to stand up and fight for what they believed was right. By the end of the saga I couldn't help but feel that rugged individuals were few and far between and that they were grossly outnumbered by spineless and fawning sycophants.

Along with my diary and a collection of newspaper clippings, I have my memories of what occurred but few of them are happy. The campaign waged by the government and other forces at the time in support of the American-led boycott of the Moscow Olympic Games was extremely nasty and more in keeping with the actions of a totalitarian state rather than those of a democracy.

"Boycotting this Olympics is a matter of high government policy...clearly is it not much of an investment for any

sponsors…Athletes should put their personal goals aside and do as their government wishes."

Statements by Prime Minister Robert Muldoon

It's hard to believe in this day and age but the vilification of those of us who attended was to continue for a number of years afterwards. Whereas I received admiration in Australia for my stance, I received only denigration in New Zealand and only once was I ever asked to speak about the Moscow games in my own country.

There was absolutely no recognition for my, or my fellow team-members position in upholding of basic Olympic principles whereas those who had betrayed those same principles went on to administer sport in New Zealand at the highest levels for the next two decades.

I have no problem remembering what occurred 37 years ago. Every four years when the Olympic Games returns, it all comes back. Rather than being happy memories of youthful sporting achievement, they are a reminder of what I experienced; betrayal, deceit, hypocrisy and disillusionment.

You might think this couldn't happen in New Zealand.

Well think again; because it did.

My childhood

I was born in the Wellington suburb of Karori but our family moved to the Blue Mountains in Whiteman's Valley, eastern Upper Hutt, when I was aged six. We were a family of seven; Mum, Dad, my sister Maree, and my three brothers; Ron, Jack, and Jeff. I was the middle-child in our family, with an older brother and sister and two younger brothers. My father earned a living as a contractor while our mother stayed at home and looked after us which was pretty normal for most families in those days. It's sad to hear of so many people growing up in broken homes today as my childhood memories are so good.

I attended Upper Hutt Primary School and Heretaunga College where I excelled at swimming and athletics and won many school championships. I was a house captain at both primary and secondary schools. They were good schools with good teachers and they left me with many great memories. My father was a former wrestler and made all us boys do morning routines of exercise, calisthenics, squats and press ups, all of which I quite enjoyed. He believed in the old maxim that the devil makes work for idle hands so we boys were expected to work around the property and to help him with his contracting work on the weekends and during school holidays. He was a tough boss too; no whinging was tolerated, just get on and do it. This direction has stuck with me to this day.

We were encouraged to train and compete at sport, study, read and generally keep ourselves occupied. "No moping about like a motherless foal" was one of my father's favourite sayings, one which I still occasionally use today. There was a community maintained tennis court and a fresh water 25-yard swimming pool fed from a local stream just across the road from our house so we all learned to swim from an early age. All the local kids spent a lot of our summers in and around that pool, either swimming or catching water beetles and freshwater crayfish, sailing home-made rafts and building corrugated iron canoes - usually without any form of supervision from parents or anyone acting as a life guard. We could all swim a bit and nobody ever looked like drowning. Dad gave me five shillings when I swam half a mile for the first time; 34 lengths of the pool non-stop once the summer had warmed the water up a bit.

My younger brother and I trapped possums to earn pocket money with the New Zealand Forest Service paying a bounty of two shillings for a scalp of neck and ears. We would go and clear our possum traps early in the morning before catching the bus to school, then return at the end of the day to skin the possums and tack out the skins to allow them to dry. When I reached my teenage years I spent a lot of time hunting pigs and deer. We had an air-rifle range off the back porch, and I had a number of rifles hanging on the wall of my room. Our home was a bit like a hunting lodge and it was a great life for a young boy. My interest in firearms continues to this day and I still compete and coach target shooting, and have made many close friends in the sport both here and overseas.

I never fully believed the view promoted by some feminists that women are disempowered in society. My father behaved as if he was the head of the household but all us kids knew that Mum really was. I feel that the real bastion of society is the family unit and it is mothers who are responsible for creating this structure. Over the years I have observed that most outstanding young athletes come from homes with strong-willed mothers. There was a study undertaken by the International Olympic Association in Switzerland back in the 1980s verifying this but for some reason it was not widely disseminated in New Zealand and I can't but feel that it simply didn't fit the politics of the times.

Growing up and joining the real world

The 1960s and early 70s were great years in New Zealand for school leavers and for employment opportunities generally; a very different situation compared to today. I left high school in 1965 having gained my University Entrance certificate. Even before my results came out I had four job interviews lined up, two with government departments and two with private companies. All of these potential employers would have paid my university fees if my course of study aligned with their area of business, and all offered me full time employment once U.E. results came out.

When results were posted, I chose the option I thought the best, though in hindsight this possibly wasn't the best decision I've ever made. I wrote back to the other three potential employers, thanking them for their offer but declining the job. I started work as a management trainee with the Woolworths Executive Trainee Scheme. Their scheme was regarded as being among the best around at the time and quite hard to be accepted for. It also paid the highest starting salary at £12 a week, whereas most other private and government department schemes and cadetships were paying £8 - £10 a week. I stayed with Woolworths for four years and left with an excellent reference.

In 1967, I volunteered for National Service in the New Zealand Army. Back then you could either volunteer or wait for the national ballot of birthday dates, which made military service compulsory if your birthday was drawn. It consisted of fourteen weeks basic training at Waiouru and Burnham camps followed by two weeks training annually for the next couple of years with the territorials. I was not impressed with the army and had expected standards to be much more demanding than they were.

When the next government scrapped the scheme I quite happily handed in my kit, much of which had never been used. Still, I met some good blokes doing National Service and the time spent away from my job gave me time to think about life and what I really wanted to do.

In my early twenties, I married my girlfriend Kath Pacey. We were married for fourteen years and we had two beautiful daughters together, Paula and Joanne. After National Service and leaving Woolworths, I worked a season at the Gear Meat Works in Petone which paid good money. When the money I had earned was combined with our savings and a bank loan, Kath and I had enough to buy our own grocery store where I made good use of my retail training.

We worked seven days a week for two years, working 12-hour shifts with my only break being an hour's run each day to keep my fitness up. When we sold the business to begin our family, we came away with enough money to buy a house almost freehold and to have it fully furnished. On top of that we owned two cars; while I was still in my early twenties. You could still achieve this by sheer hard work and a bit of enterprise in the 1970's; New Zealand certainly was the land of opportunity.

Keith Holyoake, who had been Prime Minister from 1960 to 1971, had a favourite saying about New Zealand; "We don't know how lucky we are" which was later immortalised in the song by 'Fred Dagg'. We all laughed at Holyoake at the time but I now realise how right he was.

With the sale of our business I could now afford to concentrate on what I really wanted to do, to excel at sport, with the Olympics as my goal.

For the next eight years I worked as a commercial food salesman for General Foods and they were an excellent employer. We were very well paid and as I had a strong work ethic, I always gave the company their money's worth as an employee. I simply handed my pay-packet to my wife each week and she ran the household. I have never had any desire to accumulate wealth for the sake of it; to me, a job or a business has always just been the means to allow a person to live the life they wish to lead.

Any employment I engaged in or business I owned over the years was whatever paid the most. To me, that is what freedom is about; having the economic means to allow you to choose the lifestyle you wish to lead. General Foods paid a basic retainer and commission on sales. There were no fixed hours, it was known as "job and finish". I could fit my training in around my job which paid enough for Kath to not have to work and to be able to stay at home to look after our children.

Training

Initially I concentrated on middle-distance running which I had been good at as a junior. I was fortunate to meet a very capable coach, Mike Whelan, who had himself excelled at the marathon. Mike had been coached by the Olympic medallist Barry McGee who had in turn been coached by the legendary Arthur Lydiard.

Mike really understood Lydiard's training method whereas many other coaches and runners simply read his book without fully understanding the nuances. They assumed if you trained simply by running 100 miles a week you would succeed. Lydiard was without doubt, one of the greatest middle-distance running coaches the world has ever seen. He was really shabbily treated when he ran afoul of the NZ Athletic Association and forced to seek employment as a coach outside the country, producing champions wherever he went. As time went on, he naturally became very bitter about his treatment by Athletics New Zealand (and quite rightly so in my opinion), but that's another story…

Under Mike's coaching I had built up to running 160 km a week and was pleased with my results. We both thought I was on course to compete in the 3000m steeplechase at the 1974 Christchurch Commonwealth Games. I had won the Wellington steeplechase title, had run an excellent two-mile time in competition and had bettered the Commonwealth Games qualifying time in a time-trial. We were confident that if I stuck to Mike's Lydiard-based training schedule, I would easily qualify for the Games in the coming season.

Unfortunately, an old injury then reoccurred; a spur on the tendon of my left foot resulting from when I had badly torn the tendon in my ankle years before. If it had been treated properly at the time, I would not have had the issues with my left leg that dogged me for years. There was no such thing as 'sports medicine' in the 1960s and early 70s. Doctors were generally unsympathetic to people who trained hard and injured themselves and I got the impression that some quietly considered you to be a bit of a nut case.

Treatment generally consisted of a series of cortisone injections and if they didn't work, the advice was simply to stop subjecting your body to such stress and find another less demanding sport. I was reduced to swimming and treading water in the pool, hoping this would repair the injury as I could only manage 15 minutes running before it became too painful to continue. Naturally I was feeling pretty depressed as I saw my chances of joining the ranks of outstanding athletes this country had produced over the years rapidly disappearing.

It was not until the mid-1970s that ACC was introduced in New Zealand, this was a godsend to athletes. Suddenly physiotherapists and specialist sports doctors appeared, some of whom even knew what they were doing! Many of these specialists were pioneers in their field and were largely self-taught in the treatment of sports injuries.

My discovery

One day, flicking through an English Woman's Weekly magazine, I came across an article about a British modern pentathlete named Jim Fox who had competed with distinction at the 1972 Munich Olympics. In common with most New Zealanders at the time, I had never heard of the modern pentathlon.

The sport had been conceived by the founder of the modern Olympics, Baron Pierre de Coubertin, who wanted to include a competition that tested a variety of different disciplines as one Olympic event. After much discussion, the Olympic committee decided to adapt a competitive 18th century physical test which had been used to examine potential diplomatic couriers for the King of Sweden. Applicants had to be an outstanding horseman, a capable runner in case his horse was injured, be able to swim lakes and rivers, and be able to defend himself with a sword and with a pistol. From this Scandinavian military tradition, the modern pentathlon was born.

Though the event had been contested at every Olympics since 1912, there had never been any coverage by our sports media. As soon as I read about the disciplines involved, I knew this was the sport for me. I was already a good runner, swimmer and shooter, now I would have to learn to ride a horse and fence. I wrote to the secretary of the British Modern Pentathlon Association, a retired army general. I received a prompt reply and a wealth of information as the world body for modern pentathlon was keen to get another country affiliated. They needed 40 countries affiliated to their association to remain in the top-ten sports contested at the Olympics but had only 38. If I could attempt to get the sport up and running in New Zealand, they would do everything they could to assist.

The author running at Hutt Recreation ground

The five events that made up the modern pentathlon were as follows:

Show Jumping

Originally an equestrian cross-country event, this was changed to show-jumping in the 1960s. You complete a course on a horse you have never ridden before, supplied by the host organiser and allocated to you on a ballot system. You have 20 minutes to warm up the horse and become familiar with it before starting the 800m course. You start with 1100 points and points are deducted for each fault you (or the horse) make.

Fencing

This follows the Epée discipline where 'hits' can be on any part of the body. A round robin system of three-minute, one-hit bouts means everyone competes against each other in a series of win-or-lose duels. Winning 70% of your bouts gives you 1000 points.

Pistol shooting

Twenty rounds with a .22 pistol at a target placed 25m away, this is exposed for just 3 seconds for each shot. A score of 194 out of 200 gives 1000 points, each target point being plus or minus 22 points.

Swimming

A time-trial of 300m freestyle where a completion time of 3 minutes 50 seconds gives 1000 points, with every second more or less being plus or minus eight points.

Running

A 4000m cross-country time-trial with competitors setting off at 1-minute intervals. A time of 14 minutes gives 1000 points, with each second more or less being worth plus or minus three points.

The author riding at Pauatahanui

Setting up modern pentathlon in New Zealand

I made a lot of enquiries throughout the country but the few people who had heard of the modern pentathlon were quite negative about the chances of any New Zealander being able to break into this most-European of events. It was mainly contested by full-time athletes who were generally based with their country's military forces or in state-sponsored sports academies. I tracked down a European riding instructor, Colman d'Bolgar, who was living in New Zealand. He had represented both Poland and Germany in his youth and at the time was regarded as the leading equestrian instructor in New Zealand. He gave me some good advice and wished me well with my endeavours.

I received great encouragement from the Australian Modern Pentathlon Association, particularly from their president, the former double Olympian Neville Sayers, and from Ken Hodges, the convener of the New South Wales Police Boys clubs (similar to the Boy's Institute). Australia had been involved in the sport since the 1956 Melbourne Olympic Games and their association had some very influential and capable people involved in the administration of the sport, something that I gradually began to realise was common for modern pentathlon throughout the world. They gave me an open invitation to attend all their state and national competitions and over the subsequent years I made friendships with many Australians involved in sport, some of which continue to this day.

The executive members had basically been co-opted from each of the individual sports to form the association when Melbourne won their bid to host the Olympics. Modern pentathlon turned out to be the centre of controversy during the games when two members of the Romanian pentathlon team defected and were granted political asylum in Australia.

During the games, there was another amusing incident involving the sport; unbeknown to the organisers, the caretaker of the Melbourne Hunt Club where the riding event was to take place, had taken it upon himself to tidy up the grounds. He decided to clean up and dig out all the ponds on the grounds with an excavator, not realising that one of the ponds was part of the designated cross-country course. No one bothered to re-check the water depth in the ponds since the course had been laid several weeks previously. The net result was the first competitor and his horse completely disappearing under the water when the jump was first attempted. I'll bet that competitor never forgot his Olympics; neither I imagine did the horse!

When I started in 1974, Australia had about 20 athletes competing nationally, which were held annually at state & national championships, and they sent teams to the World Champs or the Olympics each year. A women's division was also just being introduced and one of the junior women competing was Kitty Chiller. She went on to represent Australia at the 2000 Sydney Olympics and later became the country's Chef de Mission at the 2016 Rio Olympics. Her parents were to host me in Melbourne on several occasions. Australia also currently holds the Olympic title in the women's pentathlon when Chloe Espositos won gold at Rio. Her family has long been involved in Modern Pentathlon and I remember her father as a young junior in my day.

The combined total score of all five disciplines determines your overall place. The best score I ever achieved was 5180 in an Australian competition in 1979 when some top fencers from outside the modern pentathlon fraternity had been invited to ensure the Epée was of an international standard. The best competitors in the world at the time were scoring around 5300 to 5400. My best score gave me a world ranking at the time very close to the NZOC criteria of being ranked in the top 16 in the world in your chosen sport to automatically qualify for the New Zealand Olympic team.

In more recent years a number of changes to the sport have occurred. The running and pistol shooting are now combined in a manner similar to the Winter Olympic sport of Biathlon, and a laser pistol is now used which means a proper shooting range is no longer required. The swim is now 200m and fencing bouts are reduced to 1 minute each. At an international level, the standard of fencing is very high and as in any combat sport, you are only as good as your opponent will let you be. Every bout is tough with many pentathletes being good enough to represent their countries in both fencing and the modern pentathlon. Generally, they will put twice the number of training hours into fencing than any of the other individual disciplines.

At the time I was competing, the modern pentathlon was spread over five days with one event each day, but now the whole competition is run over just three days with a 'finals' section for fencing. Today it's an organiser's nightmare finding a suitable venue, but it has also made the whole event much more spectator-friendly and it received good television coverage during the 2016 Rio Olympics.

So, with the help of a few friends and sporting associates, we formed the New Zealand Modern Pentathlon Association.

A good friend, John Clark, became president and I stepped into the role of secretary-treasurer. Our committee consisted of: Richard Peterson, a Wellington lawyer and one of the country's best-ever fencers; Bruce McMillan, a top pistol shooter who had competed internationally and had won a medal at the Christchurch Commonwealth Games; and Roy Dutton, an Olympic selector and NZOC member who also became our patron. Long-time running mates, Cooky, Daryl and Mike from the Kapiti Harriers club assisted me with introductory events and the New Zealand Equestrian Association helped me with a series of riding lessons. Without the help of all these people, the establishment of modern pentathlon in New Zealand would never have occurred.

Selection

In late 1979, I was selected for the New Zealand Olympic team to contest the XXII Olympiad to be held in Moscow during the northern hemisphere summer of 1980. I was the first New Zealander ever to be selected to compete in the modern pentathlon. Like many athletes who get to compete at an Olympics, I had started to dream of this goal during my teenage years. To match yourself against the best in the world and win a medal at the Olympics; the same dream that every past, present and future competitor has ever had. It's the pinnacle of all sports competitions; just to qualify takes many years of dedication and hard work and in the case of the modern pentathlon you have to be particularly determined to excel at five different disciplines. Because of the amount of time required to reach these levels, pentathletes are often slightly older than athletes who specialise in the individual sports.

The ancient Greek's creed was;

'It is noble to compete, to pit yourself against the best and to find your true worth.'

It's what I believed in, and still do. A healthy mind in a healthy body. Compete for the love of the sport and may the best person win. No monetary prizes, no funding, no drugs.

This was the code shared by most athletes until the late 1970s when money was introduced into amateur sport and everything changed. Sport was my religion and as every Olympian knows, you have to be single-minded and fanatical about your training and competing to succeed.

Something I learnt very early on by observing international athletes involved in the pentathlon was the importance of seeking out the best coaches available. You soon got very good at working out which training programs got results, which coaches knew what they were talking about and which were time-wasters (however well-intentioned they may have been).

The best coaches are often not very popular with sport administrators, in part because they expect the same high standards from their administrators as they demand of their athletes; unfortunately, they don't always get it. Great coaches often have no time for politics and find it difficult to tolerate those who do. Many of the world's best coaches end up having huge battles with their sport's senior administrators.

Some aspiring athletes are directed towards top-level coaches who have gained their positions through holding the same points of view as their administrators rather than because of their coaching abilities.

When a nominated athlete goes before an Olympic selection panel, the selectors have all their documented performance history already before them. You must have a world ranking in the top-16 of your sport to automatically qualify for a NZ Olympic team as an 'A' category athlete.

If you have demonstrated international competitiveness and achieved a world ranking close to this criterion, you might be selected as a 'B' category athlete. Many outstanding Olympic medallists were initially selected as 'B' category athletes and proved the selectors right by performing well above expectations.

Sometimes selectors will take a punt on a young athlete who shows great potential, just to 'blood them' at their first Olympics, allowing them to gain valuable experience. A nominee for the Olympic team is closely vetted as to their current form, training programme, preparation, diet, health, and particularly their planned pre-games competition which is essential leading up to the Olympics. Rest assured, you cannot bullshit your way into an Olympic team; at least not as a competitor.

Unfortunately, more recently I've noticed that it sometimes appears that some people buy their way in as some sort of 'official'. Once you are selected you are required to sign a contract, which among other things, forbids you to speak to the media about anything to do with the Olympic team. This is deemed to be the exclusive domain of the NZOC spokesperson unless an athlete has expressly been given permission.

This may help to explain why when things started to go wrong for the 1980 NZ Olympic team, most athletes said nothing until it was too late. They simply assumed they weren't permitted to speak out and incorrectly assumed that officials would do this on their behalf.

Funding

During my entire sporting career, leading up to the 1980 Olympics, I never received a single dollar in direct funding from any New Zealand source. The sole exception was the New Zealand Horse Society (later to become the New Zealand Equestrian Federation) who sponsored me with ten free lessons after which they were at my own expense.

The world body for modern pentathlon in Sweden sent me a travel grant to attend the World Championships in Hungary. I shared the grant with John Clark who had become my manager and it paid about half of our costs. Later the same organisation gifted our association two Swiss-made target pistols.

People involved or connected with the Australian Modern Pentathlon Association often hosted me when I competed in Australian competitions and I was always made to feel welcome there, even when various states were arguing among themselves; (fierce inter-state politics in all aspects of life seems to be the norm in Australia). Everything else came out of my own pocket. With John's help, I bought and sold the odd motor car and the profit made was added to the kitty. I was a true amateur as were most athletes at the time with all Olympic sport being governed by the amateur code until the 1980s.

There was no direct funding of athletes, and no payments or prize money was permitted. Even training and travel grants were strictly controlled with severe penalties for infringements. One of New Zealand's top skiers of this era lost his amateur status and was banned from competing for two years just for appearing in an advertisement for ski goggles.

Most of the overseas competitors I got to know were based in military, police or state-run sports academies. They were paid as if they were employed full-time but actually just trained for sport. Many of those with military or police backgrounds received a promotion (and thus a higher salary) each time they were successful in competition.

Those operating within state-run sports academies often studied a unit of a physical education degree each year, the idea being that when they reached the end of their time as competitive athletes, they had graduated with a sports degree and could then begin a career in coaching. I really envied the opportunities they had and grabbed any chance I had to make use of their training facilities when I was competing internationally. These training centres often had a very welcoming 'open door' policy towards athletes visiting from what they regarded as 'developing nations'. Naturally, this all changed once you became a threat to their own competitors!

I received numerous invitations to train with teams from the United States, West Germany, Hungary and Russia and had I been a few years younger, I would have leaped at the opportunities that were offered.

From 1976 through to 1979, I progressively managed to improve my world ranking with each international competition. Starting at 44th in 1976, competing against full- time athletes I improved to 39th, then 32nd, then 24th, and finally got down to 18th at the start of the European season just prior to selection in 1979. I never doubted I had the ability to get to the top; I just wish I had learned of the sport and taken it up earlier in my athletic career.

Training

Back in New Zealand, a normal week of training was anywhere between 15-20 hours a week which I fitted in around work. A typical week Monday to Friday was as follows;

6.00am – 7.00am   Swimming with Dave Henderson's squad at Tawa Pool.

7.15am – 12.00pm   Work.

12.00pm – 12.45pm   Running at the Hutt Recreation Ground with a group of good, competitive lunch-time runners.

1.00pm – 3.30pm   Work.

4.00pm - …   Horse riding at Pauatahanui,

…then home for dinner.

As for the evenings, I'd spend two hours fencing twice a week at the Wellington Swords Club. Otherwise I spent time practicing fencing drills and air pistol at home in the garage.

On Saturdays, I would spend the morning fencing at Victoria University and the afternoon running with the Kapiti Harriers Club.

On Sundays, I would attend a competition in the early afternoon at the Heretaunga Pistol Club and often followed that with a cross-country run. When I could find the time, I fitted in a pistol training session during the week on Bruce McMillan's private shooting range. As well as winning his medal in Rapid Fire Pistol at the 1974 Christchurch Commonwealth Games, Bruce had funded his own trips to compete internationally in Europe, so he really understood what it took to try for the top in amateur sport and gave me a lot of assistance. He also helped fast-track my pistol firearms licence which can be a lengthy process to obtain in New Zealand. It was a very demanding schedule but I still found time to be with my family, cut the lawns and do jobs around the house.

Early in my sporting career I was invited by TV2 in Auckland to make a programme about the modern pentathlon. They had some well-known competitors from the different disciplines that make up the event lined up against me including the distance runner and former Olympian, Bill Baillie.

Roy Dutton and I travelled north and were hosted by the president of the Auckland Horse Society, John Hitchings. On seeing my riding, I recall him saying "If this guy is going to represent New Zealand overseas, then his riding needs some help!"

Subsequently, he arranged for the NZ Riding Association to offer me some tuition from two approved instructors, Margaret Harris and Judy Whitaker based in Waikanae. I also received a lot of help from two other instructors, Stella Harley and Tess Sturgess. I remember being told "You will be riding a proven horse. Set the horse up for the jump, give it the right signals, go with it and show confidence. If the horse fails a jump, it's your fault".

This proved to be correct and the fact that I always scored maximum or near maximum points in the equestrian section in competition is a testament to the high standard of tuition and advice these instructors gave me.

International politics, preparation and pressure

"National Olympic committees must be autonomous and must resist all pressures of any kind whatsoever, whether of a political, religious or economic nature"

Rule 24 C of the Olympic Charter.

In late December 1979, the Soviet Union invaded Afghanistan to support an unstable Soviet-friendly communist government. There were striking similarities in what was happening in Afghanistan with the actions of the United States in South Vietnam fifteen years earlier. The president of the United States, Jimmy Carter, looked for a soft option to protest against the Soviet invasion and called for an international boycott of the XXII Summer Olympics which were to be held in Moscow in July the following year.

At first this call was strongly rejected by the Olympic committees of virtually every affiliated country (including even the United States) who all saw it as a violation of rule 24c of the Olympic charter. In a brave act of defiance, a delegation of American Olympic athletes ambushed the president at a news conference and attempted to present a petition stating they still wished to compete in Moscow which had been signed by most of the US team.

Sadly, the petition was ignored and it received little media attention. Following the initial rejection of a boycott call, the pressure from the U.S. government really went on and a direct and rather nasty 'spin' campaign began in earnest. The New Zealand government responded by offering their support for Washington's view but the New Zealand Olympic Committee (NZOC) initially soundly rejected the call for a boycott after a vote was taken.

My preparation for the games had been going well. I had clipped six seconds off my swim time and had started to use 'VO2 max' type training to improve my running. I was fencing well against some top-level fencers and had just purchased a new Sako target pistol from Finland which I really liked. On top of this, I was receiving excellent treatment for the asthma I had suffered from for many years and this greatly improved my stamina.

I was planning on making use of opportunities to train with other members of the New Zealand team competing in the individual sports that make up the pentathlon, and had arranged to attend pre-games competitions in the UK and France. Everything was structured in order for me to peak at Moscow and though I knew my chances of winning a medal weren't great, I was confident I would justify my selection and have my best-ever performance at the Olympics.

Then everything started to fall apart.

Prime Minister Robert Muldoon was arguably the closest thing to a dictator this country has ever experienced. I recall how he regularly stood up in parliament waving a handful of papers threatening to release incriminating Security Intelligence Service information on anyone who opposed him.

On one occasion, he reduced one of his ministers, Marilyn Waring, to tears on national television after she dared to stand up against him. It was a disgraceful display of bullying and public humiliation but worse still, no one challenged him about his conduct. It was widely rumoured that all government ministers were required to sign an undated letter of resignation when they were appointed. These were kept on file, ready to be used by the Prime Minister at any time. He began to increase pressure on the NZOC to boycott the games.

Allan Highet was the government's Minister of Sport and was to be one of Muldoon's primary weapons in his battle against the athletes. Heavy pressure began to be applied, particularly against the younger swimmers and track & field athletes who were curtly told they were being disloyal to their country if they attended the games.

Because he hadn't got his way the first time around, Muldoon started to pressure sports officials with the strong support of Harry Julian, the NZOC yachting delegate. Julian claimed that, "only communist aligned countries, fellow travellers and Black nations are going to this Olympics".

I recall wondering where he thought the UK and Australian Olympic teams (who were going) and the Kenyan team (who weren't) fitted into this logic. He led the call for a second vote… then another… and another; five times in total. After each vote, more athletes withdrew and those remaining became more and more disillusioned. The hypocrisy and propaganda coming from the government was breathtaking. Our country's substantial trade with the Soviet Union continued unabated while athletes were being labelled communist 'fellow travellers' for wishing to compete in the same nation. As I was secretary of our association, I got to read all the minutes of the NZOC meetings so was aware of what was going on, whereas most other team members knew little beyond what they heard on the news or read in the paper.

First to withdraw was yachting, despite most of the team telling their national association that they still wished to compete. This was followed by equestrian, swimming, athletics, shooting, cycling, and hockey. The final sport to withdraw was rowing, though the team fought hard against their association's decision. All the while I kept training and kept hoping that someone with a bit of kudos and leadership would stand up and say something against what was happening.

A push-back began in Australia and the fight between the Australian Olympic Committee (AOC) and their pro-boycott government became very bitter. The government finally withdrew all funding to the AOC when they refused to comply and it was only saved from financial ruin by contributions from unions, the Australian Labour Party and private business. Eventually they sent a team of 120 athletes, but after the Olympics, the AOC passed a resolution to never again seek government funding for any Olympic team unless they could truly abide by rule 24c of the Olympic charter, remain independent and politically neutral.

Through all this I kept wondering; was someone going to start the ball rolling here? No one did. Not one former Olympian, not a single politician from any party, not one prominent person in New Zealand said anything!

Were all my years of training going to be for nothing? I remember phoning the Olympic selector, Roy Dutton, after the third vote to tell him that I would not be withdrawing from the team. He was depressed about what was happening and had just received a call from the NZ Cycling Association saying they were withdrawing their athletes' due to the threats and pressure being placed on them. He was very pleased to get my call as until then, every time his phone rang it was more bad news. I have a great respect for him and the manner in which he stood up for the principles of the Olympic Charter and never wavered.

Unfortunately, after the games, Roy and I had a difference of opinion over the 1981 Springbok Tour of New Zealand. He had become the chairman of the NZOC and was also a member of HART. He wanted to add the NZOC's voice to the controversy and oppose sporting contact with South Africa. However, I firmly believed that all sporting boycotts were wrong. It can't be right on one occasion and wrong on another. They achieve little and just make politicians feel good while using athletes as blunt diplomatic weapons. At the time, I didn't realise how strongly Roy felt on the issue but I owed the NZ Rugby Union nothing as they had failed to speak out against the Olympic boycott. The irony of the situation at the time of the Springbok Tour was that the long-serving chairman of the NZRFU Ces Blazey, promoted the view that sport and politics shouldn't mix, yet only months earlier he had strongly supported the boycott of the Moscow Olympics by the NZ Athletics Association.

Bruce McMillan opposed an attempt by some senior members of the New Zealand Pistol Association (NZPA) and the New Zealand Shooting Federation to have me expelled from the NZPA. This would have resulted in my endorsed firearms licence being revoked by the NZ Police which would have prevented me from legally owning a target pistol and thus competing at the Olympics. The committees of both associations fully supported the boycott and they sent me a rather nasty letter stating their views, although the broader membership of the two bodies were never consulted.

In later years, I was to serve on a couple of committees with some of these members; not one of them had the courage to speak to me directly about what had happened and I can't help but feel that they were too ashamed of what they had tried to do. I really respected Bruce for the manner in which he supported me when it put him offside with many of his associates in the sport.

Don Judd from the Petone Rugby Club supported my stance and even arranged for his club to send me a small donation, just as they had always done in the past when any local citizen had been selected to compete at the Olympics. He later told me that he wasn't very popular with many members of his rugby club after that.

Meanwhile, John 'Clarky' Clark was receiving a lot of criticism for his anti-boycott stance from a number of people in the Mana Yacht Club where he was a member. As well as being my manager and the president of the NZ Modern Pentathlon Association, he was a close friend. We first met working at the Gear Meat Works in Petone, both of us hoping to earn enough for a deposit on different business ventures. John was an extremely capable, generous and likable guy. He had served his time at sea and was a qualified marine engineer; there was never a dull moment when John was around. Tragically, a few years after the games he vanished along with his crew when his yacht Sequoia mysteriously sank during a storm in the Tasman Sea while returning from the Auckland - Mooloolaba race. No trace of the yacht crew was ever found.

Finally, the only sports still planning to attend the Olympics were canoeing and modern pentathlon. Richard Peterson was not only a superb fencer and my Epee coach, he was also the representative on the NZOC for both modern pentathlon and fencing. When it came to the fifth and final vote by the NZOC on whether any athletes would attend the games, Richard was able to put up two hands in favour of going, one for each of the sports he represented. This was enough to give a slim majority in favour of attending with the final vote being 8 - 7. I was so thankful to Richard for how he stood up for the Olympic charter when so many other sports officials did not.

TVNZ was planning a discussion programme about the boycott and had asked the runner and Olympian Rod Dixon to appear on behalf of the athletes; something he declined to do. He was about to leave the country and in his own words, he had had a "gutsful of the whole thing".

Having lost their star attraction, TVNZ invited me, a relatively unknown athlete, to take his place and at the last minute I agreed. I quickly realised that the whole programme was a 'stitch-up' designed to support the government's view and the pro-boycott lobby. Other than myself, the panel was made up of various political activists, academics and theologians, all of whom seemed to have an axe to grind with the Soviet Union.

The implication was that anyone who attended the games was condoning Stalin's purges, the suppression of dissidents, the persecution of religious minorities and everything else bad about the USSR they could possibly think of. The Olympic charter was never mentioned. I had expected some sort of balanced discussion but as the show progressed I grew increasingly angry. Finally, I told them what I thought of their opinions; "If you folks feel that strongly about the Soviet Union's invasion of Afghanistan, why don't you buy a rifle and plane ticket, and go there and fight instead of sitting safely back here in New Zealand, asking athletes to fight your battles for you?" It was not what they wanted to hear.

From that point on, I became the public spokesman for what was left of the team. As I was still training hard, this wasn't a role I wanted but someone needed to oppose the pro-boycott steamroller. I had assumed that Lance Cross would take on this role; as well as being chairman of the NZOC, he was a member of the International Olympic Committee (IOC) and had been elected to their executive board in 1979. What I didn't realise at the time was that he strongly supported the boycott and had placed the view of the Muldoon government before his responsibilities as an IOC member. I sometimes wonder if this might have played a part in him subsequently being awarded a knighthood.

The pressure increases

After the fifth vote by the NZOC in favour of going, I remained the only athlete of the team who was still in New Zealand. The canoeists had left earlier to train in Europe and their association had deliberately withheld their exact location from the media. As such, I became the prime target for all the pressure coming from the government, media and the pro-boycott public.

Threatening letters starting arriving in my mailbox and late night abusive phone calls began and quickly intensified, though thankfully these were outnumbered by messages of support. The worst calls always came late at night and it got to the stage where we simply left the phone off the hook in the evenings. The abusive and threatening letters (one of which was written in its author's own blood) often contained references to "God" or "treason" and these normally went straight into the rubbish bin as did the bomb threats.

Those that supported me and who had expressed their goodwill often included a small donation. This was an old Kiwi tradition going back many decades when Olympians often had to fund their own travel expenses to attend the games. I made a point of depositing any donations straight into our association's bank account in case someone was conspiring to use these financial contributions to threaten my amateur status. My wife assisted me by sending back a letter in acknowledgment which acted like a receipt and helped give me a degree of protection.

To all those people who wrote or tried to ring me at the time to offer their support, I express my heart-felt thanks. To be honest, after returning from the games I seldom replied to the letters I received, so if you were one of those who wrote, I apologise. I guess I was just too shocked by the whole experience and was consumed with an overwhelming sense of bitterness.

I was starting to feel very lonely and exposed but all of those who expressed their support helped my resolve to stick it out. However, the threatening letters and phone calls started to have an effect. I kept a loaded hunting rifle in the airing cupboard by the back door and always had an axe close to hand in the house.

Late one night there was a knock on the back door. I went out the front door and walked around so I could approach the person in the dark from behind with my axe over my shoulder. It turned out only to be my next door neighbour enquiring about one thing or another so we both pretended that me turning up in the dark with an axe was quite normal behaviour and we had a friendly conversation.

Another evening I was surprised by a knock at the front door which I opened with one hand, the other holding my hunting rifle just out of sight. It was three men from the local branch of the Labour Party. They had read an interview with me in the newspaper which mentioned that when I was asked about my politics, I stated that I was a member of the Pukerua Bay branch of the Labour Party. Surprised, they had checked their records to see that indeed this was true. In reality, my involvement in politics was negligible. I think I had attended two meetings to listen to Mike Moore and Bob Tizard and paid a $5 subscription each year and that was the total sum of it.

They told me that their branch didn't support the boycott and couldn't understand why the Labour leader Bill Rowling and the party caucus were doing so. They offered their best wishes and departed. While I welcomed the support of these local members, I felt totally betrayed by the broader party and have never voted Labour since. In later years, I sometimes made a protest vote by voting for the McGillicuddy Serious Party and also voted a couple of times for Richard Prebble as he was the only politician who finally stood up to Muldoon in parliament and told him to stop bullying athletes who wanted to attend the games.

There were only a couple of 'Newths' registered in the local phone book at the time as my surname is fairly unusual. It's actually of Welsh origin; two Newth brothers arrived in Nelson in 1840, their families following a year later. One then moved to Foxton to establish the Manawatu branch of the family that I stem from. Unusually, there was a woman with the same surname also living in our coastal community of Pukerua Bay. Though I don't recall ever having met her, neighbours later told me that she received some of the hate mail and phone calls intended for me, something I'm sure she could have done without.

The Sports Foundation

The Sports Foundation had been established in the year before the Moscow Olympics to assist athletes in their endeavours to attain top performances overseas. As I regularly competed against international athletes supported by their country's sports academies, I thought something of this nature was an excellent idea and long overdue in New Zealand. However, it had virtually no funds until in 1980, the National government offered them $80,000 for distribution to athletes who had withdrawn from the Olympics but who still wanted to compete internationally elsewhere. At that point, the Sports Foundation essentially became a tool of the government and started pressuring young athletes to withdraw from the team.

A number of news reporters I was friendly with at the time told me how most of the attacks against me in the media had originated from within the organisation which then was being principally led by Keith Hancox, a former distance swimmer and sports administrator. Interestingly, a few weeks after the Moscow Olympics had concluded I received a call from the sports journalist Hedley Mortlock. He told me he had received a tip-off informing him Hancox had taken the government's $80,000 grant and had used the money to buy a house. His source did not wish to be identified; would I be interested in leaking the story?

Coincidently, just two days earlier I had given a lift to an elderly lady whose car had broken down in the Paremata Railway Station car park. While we were chatting, she told me that her son "the well-known Keith Hancox" had just bought a house in the area and it was there that I eventually dropped her off. She was obviously quite proud of her son so I didn't mention who I was or what I thought of him.

When Mortlock told me what Hancox had done I was able to reply that not only did I already know, I even knew where the house was! However, at the time I was so traumatised by my recent experiences that all I wanted to do was avoid the lime light and declined to be involved.

The scandal was never made public but I believe a member of the Sports Foundation resigned in disgust. A prominent sports administrator was appointed to the Foundation's board by the Government and the whole episode was white-washed with the missing $80,000 explained away as being a temporary "bridging-finance loan" to Hancox. Years later, Keith Hancox and the Sports Foundation where he had become executive director were investigated by the Serious Fraud Office. He was discovered to have embezzled more than $1,000,000 from its accounts and in 1992 was sentenced to four years in prison.

In such a relatively small organisation, it seems implausible that one person could defraud it by such a large amount without others looking the other way. Unfortunately, this is not uncommon with sources of sports funding in New Zealand; anyone who asks too many questions doesn't get funded and this opens the system up to corruption. Tellingly, the tip-off that eventually resulted in Hancox's downfall came from outside the sports community.

Getting angry

With canoeing team now in Europe, much of the pro-boycott propaganda began to be directed to me. Around this time Robert Muldoon stated that "athletes should put aside their personal goals, and do as their government wishes".

Soon after I was phoned by a radio journalist for a live interview; I think it was Colin McKenzie who I always got on well with, and he asked me to respond to the prime minister's statement. It was early in the morning, I had just finished swim training and was feeling physically tired and mentally exhausted after being harassed day and night. I think my reply was along the lines of "The only guy in history who understood politicians was Guy Fawkes … and as far as I was concerned the Government could get stuffed". To say something like that today in a public forum might result in a few raised eyebrows, but to make such a statement in a radio broadcast in 1980 was extraordinary.

Lance Davidson, a friend I met after the games through masters swimming, told me how his whole office at the Ministry of Works had been listening to the interview live on the radio and no one could believe what I had just said. Quite simply no one said those sorts of things in those days – well, at least not publicly. Later, he would always jokingly introduce me to friends as "the guy who told the government to get stuffed".

Soon after the interview I received a call from New Zealand's Chef de Mission Tay Wilson saying perhaps I should tone things down a bit despite what I felt. Subsequently, every reporter who talked to me afterwards always tried to get me to repeat my statement but I kept my mouth shut.

My comment was perhaps a wee bit strong but understandable in light of what had happened just the day before. Allan Highet, who was also Minister of Internal Affairs, had approached the CEO (then called the 'Managing Director') of General Foods where I had been employed for eight years and essentially requested that he fire me. His comment to the firm was "Was it in the best interest of a major New Zealand company to employ an individual, who was defying the Government?"

The CEO forwarded the request over to the branch of the company where I worked and left the decision to them. I was called into a meeting with management and was told directly of the government's wishes. To their credit, the company stood by me and refused to action the request. I was truly grateful for their actions especially as their decision did not win them any friends within the government.

The mysterious parcel and donation

A week prior to my planned departure I received a small parcel with a covering letter of support and a small donation. All members of the original NZ team had been warned by the police not to open any parcels received in the mail due to the bomb threats. Before the cycling team had withdrawn some weeks earlier, one of the cyclists had received a suspicious looking package. The police bomb squad came to his house and blew the parcel up in his back yard. It turned out to contain his Olympic blazer (or what was left of it). It seems humorous now but the police took the bomb threats very seriously at the time.

The sender of my parcel requested me to re-post it outside of the country after I left as he suspected his mail was being intercepted. There was no way I was going to act as a courier of anything for anyone, so I asked my wife to return it unopened with a note saying that it had arrived after I had already left New Zealand. I had no idea what it contained but I strongly suspect that it was another attempt to discredit me.

The same week as the parcel incident, an article appeared in the Dominion about how I had received a $3000 donation from a guy by the name of "Morgan" who represented the Drivers' Union. This was a large sum of money which at the time would have been more than enough for a deposit on a decent-sized house. The first I knew of this was when I arrived at work one morning and was asked to go directly to the general manager's office where they placed a copy of the newspaper in front of me. I was dumbfounded. The article also included a number of fabricated comments allegedly made by me, some of which attacked my employer. The company had always supported me; would I please explain?

I was speechless. It read like an interview making out I was an agitator being paid by the USSR and that I was advocating a hard-left political doctrine. It was exactly what my opponents wanted to hear. I immediately rang the Dominion and asked to speak to the journalist who had written the article. Usually journalists are keen to have a by-line on their reports but this time it was absent; no one seemed to know who had written the article.

It turned out that there was a genuine offer of a donation which I knew nothing about at the time but this had been written about as if it had already been made and accepted. I told whoever I was speaking to that I would not be accepting the donation, it wasn't needed, and that sport had nothing to do with politics. They printed my comments the next day but using noticeably smaller font. Despite this incident, I generally had a good relationship with Wellington-based sports journalists, many of whom I knew personally and who were largely sympathetic to my stance. They were very different from the Auckland-based journalists, most of whom I had never met and who were unrelenting in their attacks.

I wrote a brief letter to Mr Morgan, thanking the union for the donation offer which I believe was genuinely made, but declining it and adding that I felt the Olympics had nothing to do with politics. He replied with a quote he attributed to Karl Marx: "Politics is the very air we breathe". I was furious; his claim of being a spokesperson for me came very close to sinking my Olympic dream.

The frame-up

Two days after the offer from the Drivers' Union, a message was left for me at work asking me to call in to the Lower Hutt police station. I assumed this had something to do with the threats I had been receiving and the warnings by police not to open any parcels sent to me. On arriving at the police station, I discovered that this wasn't the case at all; I was suspected of cashing a stolen cheque for $1000 using a forged signature at a local bank.

The interview went on for close to two hours, during which they took multiple samples of my handwriting which were taken away for analysis. I explained repeatedly that I believed the whole thing was a set-up; even in those days a bank would never have cashed a cheque for such a large amount without proper identification being presented. At one point, I could hear a couple of policemen arguing outside the interview room until eventually one of them asked me if I was "that guy going to the Olympics". When this was confirmed, his attitude quickly changed. He apologised and said he didn't know how I had become a suspect or how the whole thing had come about.

I didn't have the slightest doubt how it had come about; it was another turn of the ratchet designed to increase the pressure on me until I withdrew from the team. I expected the incident to be reported in the newspaper the following day but thankfully it was absent.

Leaving

I've never believed in turning the other cheek when someone has a go at you. Never dish out unwarranted crap to anyone, and never take it from anyone. If you give your word on something, you keep it. However, nothing had prepared me for what I was now facing and things were starting to get seriously out of hand. On top of everything else that had been happening, I now strongly suspected that my phone was being tapped. There would be a distinct "click" on my phone line shortly after a conversation began and another "click" a few minutes later.

Tay Wilson and Roy Dutton were experiencing exactly the same thing on their phones. It stopped happening immediately after a reporter from the Dominion heard it himself when talking to me on the phone and reported it the following day in the newspaper. However, the episode of being detained at the police station was the last straw. I knew that if I didn't get out of the country quickly it was going to get much worse and I was reaching the end of my tether. I went and saw my manager John Clark and we discussed the situation. He admitted he had been receiving a huge amount of criticism from so called 'friends' and was thinking about pulling out of the team. We talked and collectively decided that we had to act immediately.

Any Olympic team is divided into two sections; an advance party who goes early to set up facilities at the village and to check venues, followed by the full team which leaves about ten days later in one or more groups. I contacted Roy Dutton and asked if John and I could leave with the advance party. Roy said the NZOC still had an open booking with Air New Zealand for the original full-sized advance party and leaving with them would be no problem. My bags were already packed, we told no one other than our families and one day later we were gone.

The advance party consisted of Chef de Mission, Tay Wilson, team doctor, Dr Campbell, John Clark, and myself. Initially we couldn't decide if we should risk wearing our formal Olympic uniforms at the airport but finally decided to don our team blazers and ties as a mark of defiant pride and to hell with any consequences.

We genuinely expected an incident, perhaps getting stopped by Customs & Immigration staff but nothing happened. We hardly got a look from anyone, in part I suspect because the media hadn't been told we were leaving early. As the plane left the ground I remember experiencing the most intense feeling of relief, it felt as if a huge weight had been lifted off me. We were on our way.

John and I had a week to spend in the UK before traveling on to Moscow. We had no plans. My carefully arranged schedule for pre-games competition and training was in tatters. We stayed a night in London and met up with a couple of New Zealanders that I had previously fenced with in Wellington, Don McCrae and Leslie Calver. They had moved to London to further their fencing careers and were competing on the European circuit. We spent an enjoyable evening socialising with the local fencing community; it was such a relief not to be treated like pariahs as we had been at home.

They filled us in with what had been happening in the UK. After a bitter battle with Margaret Thatcher, the UK Olympic team had stood firm and was still going to Moscow. Only a small number of members had withdrawn, mainly from the equestrian team. They were extremely lucky to have Lord Michael Morris Killanan as the IOC president who was highly influential and strongly supported any athletes who wished to attend. Although he had inherited his title as a member of the AngloIrish aristocracy aged only 14, he had gone on to have an outstanding career as a journalist, a military officer and as a sports administrator. He was a man of great principle who strongly upheld the Olympic ideals. The only concession to the call for a boycott from the UK government was an agreement that the Olympic team would not play 'God Save the Queen' at official occasions and medal presentations and that it would be substituted by the Olympic Hymn.

The following day John contacted an old shipmate who lived in Cornwall, Jean Lavis, who invited us to spend a few days with his family in Portsmouth. They were wonderful people and made us feel very welcome. I went for a couple of training runs and a bit of a swim but generally I was overwhelmed with a feeling of mental and physical exhaustion. The main memory I have of my last-minute preparation for the Olympic Games was being introduced to scrumpy cider.

Arriving in Moscow

John, Tay, Dr Campbell and I flew together from London to Moscow. It was a bit chaotic when we arrived at Moscow airport with the arrival of different teams and supporters. We were greeted by officials and a lot of people giving instructions in regards to customs clearance and transport to the Olympic village.

I had my target pistol in my luggage and I knew I had to hand this over to an official at the airport. It's standard practice at international events for target pistols and rifles to be held in a central armoury and delivered to the range prior to practice sessions or competitions. One interpreter said someone would be along directly to take my pistol but in the confusion, he never appeared. The next minute came an announcement that our bus to the Olympic village was about to leave and so I jumped on board with everyone else.

At the village, security was very tight. There were dozens of armed guards standing in rows back to back with just enough room for people to pass between them one at a time to be scrutinised. All our baggage was being x-rayed on one of four conveyor belts. I tried to explain that I still had my pistol in my luggage which should have been collected at the airport but to no avail. It duly went through the x-ray where lo and behold, it was 'discovered' and a bit of a furore erupted.

I was interviewed by two senior-ranked security officers and asked to explain myself via an interpreter. Still not being happy with this, I was asked to give a full written statement. With everything that I had been through I had quite frankly had enough of officialdom and was not prepared to put up with any more. I simply wrote "Too many Chiefs, not enough Indians", and signed it. Once interpreted, there was a brief discussion in Russian between the interpreter and the military officers, followed by some eye rolling and nodding of heads. It seemed as if they were saying that they had warned superiors this might occur and not been listened to… and that seemed to be the end of the matter.

Every target shooter who has ever travelled to compete internationally will have similar stories to tell. Traveling with sporting firearms has always been fraught with complications, even when you have all the correct documentation, and even back in 1980 when security concerns were much lower than they are today.

At last I entered the village. Our team of eight was complimented by John Frampton who had arrived well in advance as the mechanic for the rowing team before they were forced to withdraw at the last minute by the NZ Rowing Association. Thus, we were a group of nine being accommodated in facilities which had been arranged for a full team of over 120. With our facilities came the exclusive use of four interpreters, two chauffeur driven cars and two mini buses. That said, to some extent we were on our own as the New Zealand Embassy in Moscow was instructed to avoid having any contact with us.

For the first time, we were actually together as a team. Ian Ferguson was the only team member I knew as he had tried modern pentathlon at a couple of mini-events I had organised in Wellington; just four sports with the riding excluded. I recall that while we were setting up the targets for the pistol shooting, Ian picked up a bullet, threw it at the target, and scored a nine. It was his best shot of the day! However it was the first time I had met the other canoeists, Alan Thompson, Geoff Walker and their manager John Grant. These men, all of whom I greatly respected for their stance and efforts to attend the games voted to give me the honour of being the New Zealand Olympic Team flag bearer. To be nominated by your fellow Olympians as the flag bearer for your country is one of the greatest honours any athlete can receive from his team. As we were not permitted to carry the New Zealand flag, we were to march with a black flag with a large silver fern over top of the five Olympic rings.

The opening ceremony

Only five of us marched in the opening ceremony; Tay Wilson, John Clark, John Grant, Alan Thompson and myself. Ian Ferguson decided not to march after his wife back in Auckland had received violent threats if he were to do so, and anyway, Ian and Geoff Walker had their canoeing heats beginning the following day. I also had the draw for which horse I would ride but I felt that taking part in that opening ceremony was too important an event to miss. For me it had become an act of defiance against everyone who had tried to make me withdraw and who had supported the boycott.

The opening ceremony was a huge, colourful extravaganza. The Russians are great at organising massive parades and it really showed with hundreds of gymnasts and Cossack dancers performing. A large section of the crowd created an enormous animated picture using different coloured boards which they turned in a coordinated manner; it was very well done indeed. I've watched the opening and closing ceremonies on television of every Olympics since and none of them come close to matching the Moscow Games, all of which was done without the use of high-tech lighting or other special effects. If medals were ever awarded for the opening and closing ceremonies for all Olympics, Moscow would win gold by a big margin. This amazing spectacle was never televised in New Zealand as the government had banned any coverage of the games by TVNZ. Thankfully, vintage recordings of the ceremonies can now be easily found online.

When we marched in, we spotted a group of Kiwi supporters in the crowd holding up a large banner which read "New Zealand, where are you?" They were led by the former Olympic runner Bill Baillie, who had 'competed' against me all those years ago in the television programme that was produced about the modern pentathlon.

Marching in the Opening Ceremony

John Grant, John Clark, Alan Thompson, Tay Wilson, Brian Newth (Flag Bearer)

We hadn't expected to see the group there and it came as a complete surprise. They had joined an organised tour to attend the games before the boycott had gained strength, and being keen supporters and lovers of sport, they had decided to come to Moscow regardless. Later we were to be personally introduced to them all when they hosted us to a most memorable function. The overwhelming feeling, I recall from that meeting, was their disappointment that so few New Zealanders were competing.

The games

My performance was, in one word, disastrous. The interrupted preparation, constant harassment, and no pre-games competition had its effect and I was feeling mentally and physically exhausted. There was nothing left in the tank; I had no drive and no aggression left. It had all been used up in the fight to get there. I sometimes can't help but have a wry smile when I hear athletes complaining about being under too much pressure to perform, they have no idea what being truly under pressure means.

My first day was show jumping where I had a mediocre ride. The next day was fencing where I had my worst ever international performance. The third day was shooting where my new Sako pistol malfunctioned more than the number of times allowed in the rules. The fourth day was swimming, another mediocre performance. The final day was a 4000 metre run through a forest with more armed guards in it than trees. It was an extremely hot day for Moscow at around 30+ degrees Celsius and my black woollen singlet felt like an oven. What I hoped was going to be my best-ever performance turned out to be my worst; it was as if all those years of preparation had been for nothing. My competition was over after the first five days of the games programme. The only compensation was that the Olympics still had ten days left to run.

Usually at any Olympics a competitor witnesses their own event, some of the opening and closing ceremonies, and unless they are fortunate, little of anything else. Some countries will send home any athletes who finish their competition early in the programme so that they don't disrupt the concentration of those still to compete. Alternatively, team management may try to keep those who have competed (who naturally want to 'party') in a separate part of the facility. This of course inevitably leads to some 'incidents' in regards to discipline that the public never generally hear about, in part because everyone in the team will have signed a document promising to keep their mouths shut. However, for our team, things were to be very different.

Every competitor or team manager wears an individual photo ID at all times, which basically gets them into their events venue and the Olympic village but nothing else. Each team will also receive an extremely limited number of high security 'C' passes, which allows senior officials into any venue and to occupy the best seats. Whenever you watch the Olympics on TV, you will often notice there is a block of seats, all of the same colour, all in the best position, and most of them are usually empty. These seats are generally reserved for officials and IOC members and their entourages, all of whom have 'C' passes.

Being a team of only eight with facilities for 120, we ended up with four of these 'C' passes to share between us and made full use of them. We found that if we hung a 'C' pass over top of our normal athlete's ID we could walk straight past security and occupy the best seats in a venue. Once four of us were seated, one person would be nominated to gather up our passes and to walk back out past security and repeat the process bringing in another three of us. If you had a 'C' pass and walked with confidence like you owned the place, the armed guards would never stop you.

Along with our passes we had our two cars and a minibus to transport us to any venue of our choosing. We could rush from one Olympic final of one sport over to the final of another and sit down in the best seats. The passes also included entry to evening performances of the Bolshoi Ballet which we went to twice.

I was also fortunate to see the legendary duels between the British middle-distance runners, Sebastian Coe and Steve Ovett in the 800m & 1500m finals. These two top-ranked middle-distance runners had avoided competing against each other in the year before the games, so to see them finally face each other in two superb races was one of the sport's great moments. The sad thing was that these were events that New Zealand athletes should have been competing in.

I also vividly remember Daley Thompson, the wonderful British athlete winning gold in the decathlon. With the British team's concession that the national anthem wouldn't be played at the games, I'll never forget Thompson standing on the victory dais singing 'God Save the Queen' at the top of his voice to the music of the Olympic Hymn; he was such a character.

One evening John Grant, Alan and I attended the weightlifting heavyweight final which was in progress as we entered. Vasily Alekseyev, the long-standing world champion and an icon of Russian sport, was going into the games with performance statistics that so eclipsed his rivals that he declined his early qualifying lifts. In a great display of showmanship, he contested only the final three lifts at his top weight. Suddenly the hall went very quiet; Alekseyev had miscalculated badly. There was a shocked look on our usher's face as he showed us to our seats and whispered, "Alexei has failed!"

From the weightlifting we rushed to the final of men's volleyball and from there to the next closest venue to see the women's handball final. After the match had concluded and we were waiting for the medal ceremony to begin, one of the ushers came up to us and said, "I'm sure you'll be proud to know that the New Zealand IOC member will be presenting the medals!" We thought he meant our Chef de Mission Tay Wilson. Imagine our shock when the announcement came over the public-address system; "medals will be presented by the New Zealand International Olympic Committee Member, Mr Lance Cross!" We had no idea he was even in Moscow. This was the man who had done everything he could do to stop the New Zealand team attending, who had voted in support of the boycott on all five occasions. Being an IOC member is like being a member of Olympic royalty with all the privileges that comes with it. Here he was enjoying all the hospitality reserved for top IOC officials; first class travel, the best hotels, the cocktail circuit and presenting medals to winners at the Olympics Games that he had tried to destroy for us.

We had absolutely no respect for the man and the four of us loudly booed when he was introduced to the crowd which got us some funny looks from other audience members. He then had the audacity to turn up to the Olympic village the following evening with a bottle of whisky, expecting I suspect to be welcomed as 'one of the boys'.

Moscow team left to right:

B. Newth, G. Walker, I. Ferguson, T. Wilson, J. Clarke, Dr. Campbell, A. Thompson, J. Grant

Personally, I would have loved to have done what a rowing team once did to an official they intensely disliked; they suspended him by his ankles from the top floor window of their Olympic accommodation block.

Lance soon got the message and after speaking briefly with Tay, left the village. Our IOC member was supposed to be the person that athletes looked up to uphold principles of the Olympics, but he had betrayed us all. Many years later when he was interviewed about his actions regarding the boycott he claimed that he had been under "tremendous government pressure". From where I stand, nothing excused his conduct.

The closing ceremony of the Moscow Olympiad was superb, eclipsing even the opening as a spectacle. Employing our sneaky 'C' pass transfer system, we managed to get the entire NZ Olympic team, two Irish officials, three of our Russian interpreters, a couple of Australians and most of the Zimbabwean women's hockey team all seated in the best seats in the Olympic stadium. We were never questioned but did receive a few strange looks from some of the officials seated nearby.

And so my Olympics had come to an end.

The trip home was uneventful, except for Air New Zealand charging the team for excess baggage made up of our sports gear. Air New Zealand staff apologised, but said they had been specifically instructed to do this. Tay paid the excess baggage fees for the canoes and other baggage but had some trouble getting reimbursed by the NZOC later on as certain members were so furious that we had defied them and attended the games.

Aftermath

After my battle to compete at the Olympics, I now had to face the humiliation associated with my terrible performance. It was something my critics were quick to seize upon and continued to keep talking about after returning. Anyone who says that when you are experiencing serious knock-backs, things can't get any worse is kidding themselves. Take it from me, they can! It was even raised by the yachting and swimming delegates on the NZOC that I should never have been selected in the first place.

The same people who had done everything they possibly could to obstruct and undermine my effort to attend the games now claimed I should have won a medal regardless. Eventually these critics on the NZOC were told it was time to pull their heads in and to keep their mouths shut. To this day I find it difficult to understand how people with so little understanding or knowledge of what it takes to compete at an Olympics can end up representing a sport at such a high level and unfortunately this is not uncommon even today.

The canoeists and I were still treated as pariahs and I still received hate mail. On one occasion when I was considering joining a yachting club, I was quietly told that any application for membership would be black-balled. The canoeists received similar treatment which persisted until they won gold at the 1984 Los Angeles Olympics and were suddenly transformed into national heroes.

Funnily enough, I received much more recognition in Australia than I ever did here. I was invited to speak to the chairman of the Australian Olympic Committee who congratulated me on my stand. I also had a very sympathetic interview with one of Australia's most popular radio sports hosts. He asked me, "Whatever happened to the 1980 New Zealand Olympic team?"

I replied truthfully that "it simply seems that Australians have more guts than Kiwis. You guys stood up to your politicians, even though Australia was a much stauncher ally of the United States than New Zealand was." He liked that!

In more recent years I have attended a couple of major sports functions in Australia where my wife Robyn and I have lived on and off over the years. When organisers discovered who I was, Robyn and I were invited to sit with the honoured guests and V.I.Ps. They assumed that I must have some elevated position in New Zealand sport; well far from it. At best I've been told that I was some sort of 'maverick' and while I was included in functions organised by the Olympians Club, I was never invited to any other major sports events or gatherings. The fact that a few of us had attended the Moscow games seemed to be 'air brushed' out of New Zealand sporting history for many years. To this day it still irks me to occasionally hear a poorly informed sports commentator refer to the 1980 Olympics as the one that "New Zealand did not attend".

It's such a shame that New Zealand did not have someone of the calibre of Sebastian Coe. He stood up to his government's bullying, stuck up for the Olympic Charter, competed at Moscow winning a gold medal, repeated the feat four years later at the Los Angeles Olympics, and eventually went on to become the president of the organising committee for the London Olympic Games. I have the greatest respect for the man who now deservedly occupies a seat in the House of Lords. Lord Coe now leads the fight against drugs in sport and is currently the president of the International Association of Athletics Federations.

All athletes feel they have entered a sporting vacuum after an Olympics, particularly if it marks the end of their top-level career in sport. After what I had been through, there was no way I wanted to continue with serious sporting endeavours. I recall being asked by a journalist if I intended training through to the next Olympics. I replied, "Mate, I would have to be bloody insane to risk going through all that again."

Over the following years, I half-heartedly continued with target shooting where I managed to get into the National squad on a few occasions. I joined a masters swimming group which is where I met Robyn who has been my lovely wife for the last 30 years. I also flirted with triathlon in the veteran class until I had a bad cycling accident (there are two types of people that do competitive road cycling; those that have had a bad accident and those who are going to). Today I am retired but still coach a bit of swimming for the Upper Hutt City Council swim school and compete and coach pistol shooting.

Three decades on

In 2005, 25 years after the Moscow Olympics, and with the ironic situation in place of the United States now occupying Afghanistan, it was time to say something. A new generation was now in position at the top of the NZOC and I was invited to address the association. I told them what an open wound it still was for those selected to be part of the original team and how, through no fault of their own, they had been denied the opportunity to compete and to be able to join the NZ Olympians Club for former athletes. Subsequently and to their credit, the NZOC held a reunion for those who should have been in the Moscow Olympic team.

Every original member was given a written apology for the manner in which the whole sorry mess was handled. There was even an apology read out by the then-Minister of Sport at the function held at the Olympic Committee's headquarters on Queens Wharf in Wellington. For the first time, the Olympic Museum included a display about the history of the Moscow Games. There were many speeches about the pressure that was applied at the time to athletes and officials but everything seemed to give the impression that no one had actually supported the boycott. All I can say is that those who spoke out against the boycott must have done so very quietly as I certainly would have heard them if they had.

Ian Boyd from Athletics NZ mentioned to me that Allan Highet told him, before his death in 1992, that he "deeply regretted" his actions in regards to the boycott when he had been Minister of Sport. However, his change of heart was never relayed either to the team or to the media. I couldn't help but notice that almost everyone who at the time had been directly involved in advocating for the boycott was now saying that they had originally supported the principles of the Olympic Charter but they had been hood-winked by the government.

I don't buy it. Personally, I believe that all of the officials who played a part in violating rule 24c should have been expelled from the NZOC for at least five years.

For the first time, I met some other members of the original team and learned that they too had received hate mail and threatening phone calls, all of which ceased when they withdrew from the team. I can't help but feel that there was a degree of orchestration and organisation in the manner in which these threats were made. Noticeably absent at the reunion were the remaining canoeists. I assume they have such bad memories of what occurred that they preferred to forget; I can't say I blame them.

Unfortunately (or perhaps fortunately) the gathering had to be abandoned early when an earthquake set off the building's fire alarms just as I had been invited to speak. I had intended to ask why it had taken the NZOC 25 years to fix this, why hadn't it been done years before and why had dishonourable people been protected for so long.

New Zealand Olympic Committee
Educating youth through sport and the Olympic ideal

November 2005

Dear 1980 Moscow Olympic Team Member,

As its October 2005 Meeting the NZOC Board received a submission from the Olympians Club of New Zealand (via Peter Miskimmin) to seek some formal recognition for those athletes selected for the Moscow Games, but were then withdrawn for reasons beyond their control.

The NZOC Board were unanimous in their support for this request.

The Board accepted that the NZOC should well have acted sooner to support the athletes at the time of their intense disappointment, but resolved to grant formal acknowledgment and recognition to the selected 1980 athletes, in the records of the NZOC.

No belated apology could redress the disappointment and frustration of the chosen athletes for these Games, which is acknowledged by the NZOC today.

We can only hope that those athletes who did not get an Olympic experience, can take some consolation from this belated acknowledgment, and can still reflect on a proud achievement to have been selected for the ultimate sporting event.

The NZOC is grateful for the work of the Olympians Club in presenting this matter, and will work closely with the Club to further the interest of all New Zealand's elite sportsmen and women.

With the passage of time, our contact details for the 1980 team are not necessarily complete. The attached list of names are those for whom we have no current address, and your assistance in locating them for us would be appreciated. Please advise Lorraine Kent (lorraine@olympic.org.nz or phone 04 385 0070) if you know of their whereabouts.

Kind regards

Yours sincerely

Barry Maister
Secretary General

3rd floor, Olympic House, 265 Wakefield Street, PO Box 643, Wellington, New Zealand
Tel: +64 4 385 0070   Fax: +64 4 385 0090
email: office@olympic.org.nz, Website: www.olympic.org.nz

Conclusion

If you were one of the 1980 Olympic team's victims, perhaps it's time to consider writing your own memoirs of what happened to you at the time. On the few occasions over the years that I have spoken about my experiences of the boycott, I'm sure there are always a few who believe that I'm making it all up and that something like this couldn't have happened in this country. People don't always want to hear the truth.

Of the original team, John Clark, Geoff Walker and Tay Wilson have sadly passed away. I've had a couple of health scares myself so I felt my story needed to be told even if some people might prefer that it wasn't. The bitterness arising from these actions survives among some to the present day and this revealed itself at the funeral in 2014 of our Chef de Mission who in later years had become Sir Tennent Edward Wilson, after being knighted for his services to sport.

The Wilson family had asked that the boycott not be mentioned at the service, a strange request but something I've grown used to it over the years at sport gatherings. 'Don't mention the Moscow Olympics' seems to be the mantra lest some people find their reputations tarnished. Despite the taboo, one of the rowers giving a eulogy made sure that everyone knew exactly where Tay had stood on the issue and how opposed he had been to the boycott.

So that's my story; history should be about the truth.

Brian Newth

New Zealand Olympic Team Flag Bearer, 1980

After thoughts

After being involved in competitive sport for 50 years, I have developed some opinions on topical issues which I would like to briefly share with you.

Drugs in sport

This can be summed up in one word; hypocrisy. Unfortunately, modern performance enhancing drugs work. Sports people who make their living from competing at the highest level often observe what is going on around them and are faced with the question; do I wish to compete at a top level, or do I wish to remain drug free?

Just as a large section of the population have come to accept a culture of recreational drug use, in recent years similar acceptance of performing enhancing drugs has entered sport, particularly in professional codes. There probably aren't too many gyms in this country where these drugs are not obtainable from someone.

It is extremely difficult to obtain the physiques that some sportsmen have today without their use. Growing numbers of older sports people are succumbing to rare kidney and glandular disorders caused by earlier drug use. If those involved in professional sport want to identify which of their associates might be using performance enhancing drugs, there is one thing to look for; those who use recreational drugs to 'party' will also likely be using drugs to enhance their sporting ability.

I fully support the work of Lord Coe and others to rid sport of drug cheats, but I feel they face an uphill battle unless our society as a whole has a change of attitude regarding the acceptance of drug use. I believe that only humiliation will work; as well as being banned, the names of athletes found to have used prohibited substances should appear on a permanent website as should the names of their coaches if they are found to have been complicit in the activity.

Corruption in sport

Over the past five decades I've been on the regional, national or international executive of five different sporting codes, always in a voluntary capacity. I have probably attended over a thousand committee meetings relating to these codes during that time and have built up many contacts over the years. One thing I have come to realise is that when it comes to sport, money that isn't closely audited will often disappear through fraudulent activity. However, what is even more upsetting is the amount of effort that regularly goes into covering up the actions of fraudsters.

If half the effort that goes into this went into regularly auditing an organisation's accounts, then these 'errors of judgment' would never reach the proportions they do. Every sports organisation which has large sums of money moving through its bank accounts has experienced this, sometimes several times. What amazes me is that good people who have given years of service as unpaid volunteers will join in keeping these scandals quiet from the media in the mistaken belief that exposing these thieves will (particularly if they are national figures) be damaging to their sport. This practise often means that a majority of those involved in a sport at a grass-roots level remain unaware of what has occurred or who was responsible.

The pattern always seems to be the same. Once the misappropriation of funds reaches a crisis point, someone with clout will speak out or is finally listened to. A forensic audit takes place, often accompanied with a public statement that someone has made an 'error of judgement'. Following the audit, there will be an announcement that a noted figure will be 'standing down' from their position within that organisation. This may be because they wish to 'further their career', to 'simply move on', or because they are 'retiring due to health issues' or some such similar excuse. A short time later a major restructuring of that organisation will be announced. Everyone involved in the administering of the organisation level changes job descriptions and a few months later, everything is back to normal (except for the hole in the finances).

Those who really should have been prosecuted get to keep their reputations with few consequences. Everything is arranged so as not to damage the public image of the organisation concerned and to cover-up the fact that people around the offender were turning a blind eye or were involved to some degree. Anyone who blows the whistle is shunned. If the organisation is of a considerable size, sports journalists will avoid investigating the story because of the risk they'll lose access to their contacts and athletes in that sport.

I believe that those who commit such fraud as administrative officers of any sport, should, regardless of who they are, be treated in the same manner as drug cheats. The results of any investigative audit and the names of those involved should be made publicly available; currently too many people get away with it with their reputations intact.

Brian

The author and his wife Robyn today.